KU-753-641

04133

Science In Your Life:

HOT AND COLD
FEEL IT!

Wendy Sadler

www.raintreepublishers.co.uk
Visit our website to find out more information about **Raintree** books.

To order:
☎ Phone 44 (0) 1865 888112
🖹 Send a fax to 44 (0) 1865 314091
🖥 Visit the Raintree bookshop at **www.raintreepublishers.co.uk** to browse our catalogue and order online.

First published in Great Britain by Raintree,
Halley Court, Jordan Hill, Oxford OX2 8EJ,
part of Harcourt Education.
Raintree is a registered trademark
of Harcourt Education Ltd.

© Harcourt Education Ltd 2006
The moral right of the proprietor has been asserted.

All rights reserved. No part of this publication may
be reproduced, stored in a retrieval system, or
transmitted in any form or by any means, electronic,
mechanical, photocopying, recording, or otherwise,
without either the prior written permission of the
publishers or a licence permitting restricted copying
in the United Kingdom issued by the Copyright
Licensing Agency Ltd, 90 Tottenham Court Road,
London W1T 4LP (www.cla.co.uk).

Editorial: Melanie Copland, Kate Buckingham,
and Lucy Beevor
Design: Victoria Bevan
and Bridge Creative Services Ltd
Picture Research: Hannah Taylor
and Catherine Bevan
Production: Duncan Gilbert

Originated by Chroma Graphics (Overseas) Pte. Ltd
Printed and bound in China by
South China Printing Company

ISBN 1 844 43663 2
10 09 08 07 06
10 9 8 7 6 5 4 3 2 1

**British Library Cataloguing in
Publication Data**
Sadler, Wendy
Hot and cold. – (Science in your life)
536
A full catalogue record for this book is available from
the British Library.

Acknowledgements
Alamy Images pp. 13 (BananaStock), 11 (Comstock
Images), 20 (Edward Hattersley), 15 (Elvele Images),
21 (ImageDJ), 18 (NewStock), 26 (Nick McGowan-
Lowe); Corbis pp. 14 (Barbara Peacock), 16 (Gabe
Palmer), 25 (Jim Sugar), 27 (Kevin Schafer); Corbis
Royalty Free pp. 9, 12, 22, 24; Digital Vision p. 23;
Getty Images pp. 5, 17 (PhotoDisc); Harcourt
Education Ltd pp. 4, 8, 19, 29 (Tudor Photography),
10; Photographers Direct p.7 (Yves Tzaud
Photographe).

Cover photograph of thermometer reproduced
with permission of Corbis/Thom Lang.

Every effort has been made to contact copyright
holders of any material reproduced in this book.
Any omissions will be rectified in subsequent
printings if notice is given to the publishers.

The paper used to print this book comes from
sustainable resources.

Disclaimer
All the Internet addresses (URLs) given in this book
were valid at the time of going to press. However,
due to the dynamic nature of the Internet, some
addresses may have changed, or sites may have
changed or ceased to exist since publication. While
the author and publishers regret any inconvenience
this may cause readers, no responsibility for any
such changes can be accepted by either the author
or the publishers.

An adult should supervise all of the activities in
this book.

Contents

Any words appearing in the text in bold, **like this**, are explained in the glossary.

Hot and cold things in your life

Have you noticed how hot or cold anything is today? You may have had hot porridge for breakfast, or a cold glass of orange juice. Perhaps your porridge was too hot. What could you do to make it have just the right amount of heat? The word we use to describe how much heat something has is **temperature**.

Blowing on hot porridge is one way to cool it down.

When you wash your face the water temperature needs to be just right. You can add some cold water if the water is too hot.

If your hands get very cold then your fingers do not work very well. They get stiff and they feel numb. You can warm them up by putting gloves on.

These children are outside on a very cold day. They are not too cold, because they are wrapped up warm!

What is heat?

Heat is a kind of **energy**. This energy is made by tiny **particles** called **atoms**. Everything around us is made up of atoms. The atoms are always jiggling around. As things get hot, the atoms inside start to move around more quickly.

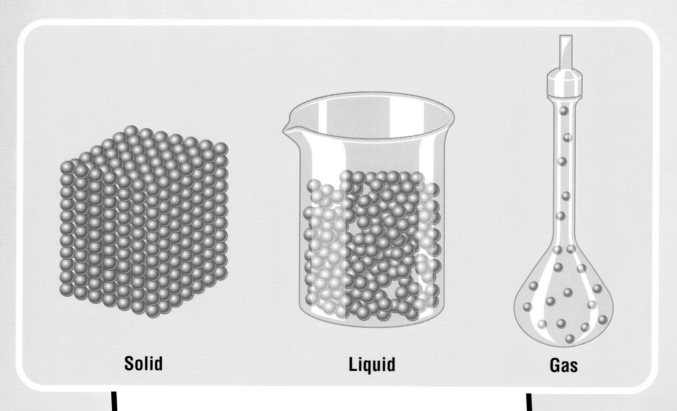

Solid   **Liquid**   **Gas**

Atoms in a solid object are packed very close together. In a liquid, the atoms are more spread out. In a gas, the atoms are far away from each other.

The red cup contains hot water and the blue cup contains iced water. Can you see how the red liquid inside the thermometers is at different levels inside the tube?

We can use a **thermometer** to measure how hot or cold something is. **Temperature** can be measured in degrees Celsius (°C) and degrees Fahrenheit (°F). Your fridge is a chilly 5 °C (41°F) and boiling water is 100 °C (212°F). To freeze water into ice it needs to get down to a temperature of 0 °C (32°F)! A nice hot bath is about 40 °C (104°F) and the **surface** of the Sun is very hot at around 5,500 °C (9,932°F)!

Heat on the move

Heat can move through solid objects. This is called **conduction**. The jiggling of the **atoms** is passed on from one place to the next until the heat has spread.

Some other objects are not good at conducting heat. These are called **insulators**. Materials such as wool, foam, and plastic are good insulators. We use insulators when we want to stop heat travelling from one place to another.

Metal is a good conductor of heat. If you put a metal spoon into a cup of hot chocolate the heat will travel along the spoon quickly.

In the kitchen we use oven gloves to pick up hot things. They stop the heat from flowing into your hand and hurting you.

When we heat water in a pan, the heat moves through the water in a different way. The hot water rises up and the cool water sinks down. The cool water then gets heated up and this carries on until all the water is hot. This is called **convection**.

Fr-fr-fr-fridges

Heat always wants to flow from a hot place to a cooler place. Sometimes we want heat to flow away from something to make it colder. Fridges, freezers, and air conditioners all have to move heat from a cold place to a warmer place.

Heat does not like to move from a cold place to a warmer place, so we need **energy** to make it move in the right direction. This is why fridges and freezers need **electricity**.

Without a fridge we would not be able to keep food cool and fresh for long.

Electricity is used to turn a special liquid inside the fridge into a gas. When liquids turn into gas we say that they **evaporate**. As they evaporate they take heat with them. By taking heat out of the fridge the fridge gets cold.

An air conditioner works in a similar way to a fridge to cool down your house.

Imagine life without fridges

Without fridges, some of our food would rot very quickly. We would waste a lot of food and we would have to go to the shops a lot more often to buy fresh food.

Body heat

Our bodies have to be at the right **temperature** to work properly. Humans are **warm-blooded** animals, which means that our bodies make heat from the food we eat. We use clothes to help keep us warm or cool so that our body temperature stays the same.

Cold-blooded animals do not make their own heat. The heat of their bodies depends on how hot or cold it is around them. Snakes and lizards are both cold-blooded animals. They have to sit in the sun for a while to get warm enough to move around.

The energy we get from food is turned into heat inside our bodies.

Inside our bodies the temperature should stay at about 37 °C (98.6°F). If we get a few degrees too hot, or too cold, we can get ill or even die.

Your heart pumps blood around your body. The blood takes heat with it. This makes sure that every part of your body stays warm. Hands and feet are a long way from your heart so they often get cold first.

A thermometer is used to measure your temperature to check you are not ill.

Keeping cosy

When the weather is cold outside we need to make sure we keep our body heat in. We use clothes that are good **insulators** to help us trap the heat. Wool is a very good insulator. You might wear a woolly hat and scarf on cold days to keep warm.

You lose a lot of heat through your head, so a hat is very important when you want to stay warm.

A woolly scarf has lots of little holes in it. These holes trap small pockets of air in the **material**. The air and the wool together are very good at trapping heat.

This walrus is a warm-blooded animal that swims in very cold water. A layer of fat keeps it warm.

Warm-blooded animals that live in cold places usually have thick fur or layers of fat to help them stay warm. Fur and fat are good insulators. When the weather gets warmer the animals lose some of the fur or fat so that they do not get too hot.

Cold-blooded animals do not need to stay at the same temperature. This is why most cold-blooded animals do not have fur or wool coats. Instead they have smooth skin or scales.

Keeping cool

When the weather is warm, or we are running around, we can get too hot. Your skin can help you to cool down by sweating. As the sweat **evaporates** it takes away some heat to help you stay cool.

Some people use electric fans to stay cool. The moving air helps to make the sweat evaporate more quickly. This makes you feel cooler.

Our bodies cool down by sweating when we are too hot.

Hot and cold in your life!

Blow on the back of your hand. Feel how this makes your skin feel cool. Now lick the back of your hand and feel the extra cooling when you blow.

If you get wet, heat from your body will be used to evaporate the water. This will happen even if you do not feel hot! This is why you may sometimes feel cold when you step out of the bath or the swimming pool.

When you are hot you should wear thin clothes that let the heat move away from your body.

African elephants lose lots of heat through their ears to help them stay cool!

Melting and boiling

Melting is what happens when solid things become a liquid. You need heat to melt things. Ice is a solid. If we add heat to the ice it will melt and become water. Ice will melt in a warm room, but other things need a lot more heat before they will become a liquid.

On a hot day you have to eat your ice cream fast before it starts to melt!

If you put more heat into a liquid it can become a gas. This is called boiling. A kettle uses **electricity** to heat water until it boils. The steam that comes out of the kettle is a gas called **water vapour**. Water can be a solid, a liquid, or a gas.

Most plastic objects are made by melting plastic and making it into shapes when it is soft. When the plastic cools down it becomes a solid again. If you look around you will find lots of different plastic shapes in your home.

Hot and cold in your life!

Put an ice cube into your mouth. Do not crunch it. Feel it melt as your body heat warms it up.

Freezing and condensing

When we take heat away from a gas it cools down. When a gas gets cold enough it can become a liquid again. This is called **condensing**.

When it is very cold outside, you sometimes see a cloud when you breathe out. The cloud that you see is made of tiny water drops that have come from a gas called **water vapour** in your **lungs**.

When water vapour moves from the warmth of the body to the cold air outside, it condenses into water.

When things freeze they are turning from a liquid into a solid. To make something freeze you have to take heat out.

When water freezes it turns into ice. Ice is a solid. Water turns into ice at 0 °C (32°F). If water freezes in clouds it can fall as hail, sleet, or snow.

When you put water into an ice tray it becomes the same shape as the holes in the tray. When water is frozen it becomes a solid and stays the shape it was when it was frozen.

The weather

Earth gets its heat **energy** from the Sun. Heat energy and light travel from the Sun, through space, to Earth. We call this **radiation**. Heat energy from the Sun keeps the Earth warm and provides the energy for all of the weather that we get on Earth.

The water on Earth is heated by the Sun and some of it **evaporates** into the sky. Here it forms clouds. When the clouds get cooler the water **condenses** back into liquid, and falls as rain.

Rainbows appear in the sky when the light from the Sun shines through raindrops.

The Sun also heats the air around Earth. When air gets hot it rises. As the air rises and the Earth turns, we get winds that can move clouds around. On hot days, the air can sometimes rise up very quickly. This can make big clouds that give us thunder and lightning.

When lightning strikes, the air gets heated up to 30,000 °C (54,032°F)! This sudden heating of the air is what makes the sound of thunder.

Cold Earth, hot Earth

Around the middle of Earth there is an **imaginary** line called the **equator**. The weather is hotter here because the sunshine is spread over a small area. Each small area gets very hot.

At the top and bottom of Earth are the North and South Poles. Here, the weather is very cold. The sun shines over a much bigger area so the heat is spread out.

It is so cold at the South Pole that the ground is made of ice and snow.

Inside the centre of Earth it is very hot indeed! It is so hot that rocks and metal can melt. This only happens deep below the Earth's crust. The crust is the **surface** of Earth.

In some parts of the world Earth's crust is very thin, and even broken. In these places the hot, melted rock can rise to the surface. This happens when a volcano erupts.

This volcano is erupting. The hot, melted rock sprays out of the volcano and on to the surface of Earth.

Heat around the house

We need different kinds of houses in hot and cold places. If it is cold, the house must have good **insulation** and double glazing in the windows.

A house can be insulated with thick foam in the walls or the roof. Double glazing is when windows are made of two sheets of glass. Air is trapped between the sheets of glass. Both of these things help to trap heat inside a house.

This window is double glazed. The air in the gap is a very good insulator.

In hot countries some houses have small windows. This stops the sunlight from heating up the rooms. Many people also paint their houses white in hot countries. This helps to keep the houses cool because it **reflects** away some of the heat from the sunlight.

Houses in hot countries are often painted white to keep them cool.

Hot and cold facts

Hot and cold things are everywhere. Sometimes we like things to be hot, and other times we want them to be cold. We heat things up and cool them down all the time. Think how hot and cold things affect your life!

Temperature can be measured in degrees Fahrenheit (°F), Celsius (°C), or Kelvin (K).

Boiling point of water	100°C/212°F
Freezing point of water	0°C/32°F
Absolute zero	−273°C/−459.4°F

Absolute zero is the name of the coldest temperature that you can get.

The hottest day ever recorded was in El Azizia in Libya. The temperature was 58°C (136°F).

Death Valley in California is a close second with temperatures up to 57°C (134°F).

The coldest place on Earth is Antarctica, with a temperature of −89.4°C (−129°F).

The temperature inside your fridge should be about 5°C (41°F).

The average body temperatures of some **warm-blooded** animals:

- humans: 37°C (98.6 °F)
- rabbit: 38.5°C (101.3 °F)
- polar bear: 37.2°C (99.1 °F)
- blue whale: 35.5°C (95.9 °F)
- ostrich: 39.2°C (102.6 °F)

Find out more

You can find out more about science in everyday life by talking to your teacher or parents. Your local library will also have books that can help. You will find the answers to many of your questions in this book. If you want to know more, you can use other books and the Internet.

Books to read

Discovering Science: Hot and Cold, Rebecca Hunter (Raintree, 2003)

Science Files: Heat and Energy, Steve Parker (Heinemann Library, 2004)

Using the Internet

Explore the Internet to find out more about hot and cold. Try using a search engine such as www.yahooligans.com or www.internet4kids.com, and type in keywords such as "Celsius", **"temperature"**, and "weather".

Glossary

atoms tiny particles that are inside everything

cold-blooded animal that needs heat from the Sun to keep it warm

condense make a gas cold so that it becomes a liquid again

conduction when heat moves through a solid

conductor when heat moves along an object by vibrations inside the material

convection when warm bits of liquid or gas move around

electricity form of energy that can be used to make things work. Computers and televisions work using electricity.

energy power to make things work. You need energy to get up and walk or run around.

equator imaginary line around the middle of Earth

evaporate when water turns from a liquid into a gas

imaginary not really there

insulator material that stops heat moving from one place to another

lungs part of your body inside your chest that you breathe into

material something that objects are made from.

particles very tiny pieces. Everything all around you is made up of particles.

radiation when heat travels through space from the Sun to Earth

reflect bounce off

surface top, or outside part of an object

temperature how hot or cold something is

thermometer tool that measures your temperature

warm-blooded animal that can make enough heat to keep itself warm

water vapour gas made up of small droplets of water

Index

Titles in the *Science In Your Life* series include:

Hardback   1 184 443658 6

Hardback   1 844 43662 4

Hardback   1 844 43659 4

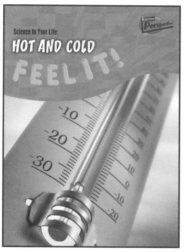

Hardback   1 844 43663 2

Hardback   1 844 43660 8

Hardback   1 844 43664 0

Hardback   1 844 43661 6

Find out about the other titles in this series on our website www.raintreepublishers.co.uk